Original title:
The Couple's Conclave

Copyright © 2024 Swan Charm
All rights reserved.

Author: Olivia Orav
ISBN HARDBACK: 978-9916-89-190-2
ISBN PAPERBACK: 978-9916-89-191-9
ISBN EBOOK: 978-9916-89-192-6

Love's Lonely Voyage

In the silence of the night,
Two hearts drift apart,
Across the shadowy sea,
A longing search for a spark.

Waves crash with each sigh,
Stars whisper a tune,
Memories like anchors weigh down,
Lost in a vast cocoon.

The moon guides the way,
Yet winds shift in despair,
Each heartbeat a compass,
Pointing to hearts laid bare.

Time dances slowly here,
Sailing toward lost dreams,
Carrying tales of love,
On worn-down, fragile beams.

Hope flickers like a flame,
In darkness, it survives,
Despite the loneliness felt,
The voyage still strives.

Reflections in a Shared Dream

Two souls interlace,
In a dance of the night,
Whispers turn to laughter,
As the stars gleam bright.

Visions weave a tale,
Of places yet unseen,
In the quiet corners,
Where hearts paint the scene.

Time bends in stillness,
As moments intertwine,
With every gentle touch,
The universe aligns.

Dreams build a bridge,
Between thoughts and desire,
In the mirrored silence,
Passions never tire.

Together they wander,
Through the fabric of sleep,
In reflections so vivid,
Their promises keep.

A Meeting of Minds

In a bustling café,
Ideas flow like wine,
Two thinkers engage,
In the warmth they find.

Words dance on the table,
Like leaves in the breeze,
Sharing vibrant thoughts,
With effortless ease.

Perspectives collide,
Yet harmony sings,
Bridging gaps through discourse,
As wisdom takes wings.

Each moment a lesson,
Each laugh a new thread,
In the tapestry woven,
Where intentions are spread.

Connections grow stronger,
Through a meeting so rare,
In the heart of the city,
Two minds lay bare.

Love in Gentle Waves

Upon the shore where shadows play,
Our hearts like tides ebb and sway.
In whispers soft, the ocean sings,
Of love that dances on fragile wings.

Moonlight bathes the quiet sand,
With every touch, we understand.
The pull of dreams, the soothing tide,
With you, my soul can safely glide.

Through stormy nights and sunny days,
Our passion flows in countless ways.
Like waves that crash and then retreat,
In every rhythm, our hearts meet.

Together strong, through rough and mild,
In every moment, forever wild.
A sea of joy, a swell of grace,
In love's embrace, we find our place.

A Haven for Two

In quiet corners, shadows blend,
We find a space where hearts can mend.
Within these walls, our dreams take flight,
A sanctuary wrapped in light.

Soft murmurs float in gentle air,
With every glance, a promise shared.
In laughter's glow, our worries cease,
Together we build our sweet release.

The world outside fades to a hush,
In this haven, time bends to us.
Every heartbeat, a whispered vow,
In this sacred place, here and now.

Through stormy nights, we find our calm,
In every touch, a healing balm.
With open arms, we welcome dawn,
In our haven, we are reborn.

Silence as the Canvas

In stillness deep, we paint with thought,
With silence hushed, a canvas caught.
Each breath we take, a stroke of art,
In quiet spaces, we find our heart.

The world can wait, our minds at ease,
In gentle whispers, our souls appease.
With every pause, a story spun,
In the realm of silence, we are one.

Beneath the stars where dreams ignite,
We sketch our hopes in the soft night light.
In tranquil hues, emotions flow,
The quiet canvas helps us grow.

With unspoken words, our spirits glide,
In silence, love will not abide.
Together we create, a work so rare,
A masterpiece born from the air.

Moments Wrapped in Time

In shadows cast by fading light,
We find the echoes of our plight.
Each second slips like grains of sand,
Embracing dreams within our hands.

Fragments of laughter softly play,
In memories we can't betray.
The clock ticks on while we hold tight,
To fleeting joy that feels so right.

With every heartbeat, moments blend,
Creating tales that never end.
Captured whispers in the night,
Promise dawn will bring new light.

Time's gentle touch, both cruel and kind,
Leaves traces in the heart and mind.
We dance on edges of the now,
In moments wrapped, we take a bow.

Where Hearts Intertwine

Beneath the stars, two souls take flight,
Their dreams collide in pure delight.
In silence shared, no need for speech,
Where hearts entwined, their hopes can reach.

The warmth of hands, a gentle trace,
In every laugh, a sacred space.
Through laughter's glow and sorrow's rain,
They find their strength through love's refrain.

Each whispered secret, soft as air,
A bond of trust, beyond compare.
In twilight's hush, they feel the spark,
A journey lit within the dark.

With every heartbeat, love's embrace,
In tangled paths, they find their place.
Together, they can face the fight,
In moments where their hearts unite.

A Canvas of Emotions

Brush strokes bold in vivid hues,
Upon the canvas, dreams diffuse.
With every splash, a story told,
Of warmth and heart, both brave and bold.

Colors dance like flickering light,
In shadows deep, they chase the night.
From joy to pain, each shade commands,
A palette rich in life's demands.

The hues of love, both bright and fair,
Blend seamlessly in tender care.
With every tear, a shade is born,
To paint the dawn, a world reborn.

In every stroke, emotions flow,
An artist's heart, a vibrant show.
The canvas waits, both wide and free,
To capture life's true tapestry.

Secrets Only We Share

In whispered tones beneath the stars,
We bare our souls, forget the scars.
A world unseen where dreams align,
In shadows deep, our secrets shine.

Each cherished word, a treasure kept,
In silent nights when others slept.
With fragile hearts, we weave our tale,
A bond unbroken, strong and frail.

The truth we hold, a sacred fire,
In every glance, our hearts conspire.
With time as witness to our plight,
We find our strength in shared twilight.

These woven threads, so fine and rare,
Create a tapestry we share.
In every secret, love runs deep,
In quiet moments, dreams we keep.

Path of Two Souls

In the twilight where shadows blend,
Two souls wander, hand in hand.
With whispers soft, and gazes deep,
They carve a path where dreams are planned.

Every step echoes through the night,
With laughter that dances in the air.
Hearts entwined, a gentle light,
Guiding them forward, free from care.

Memories weave through the soft winds,
Each moment cherished, beyond time's reach.
In the silence where love begins,
They find solace in every speech.

Beneath the stars, their stories grow,
A tapestry of fate and love.
In fields of gold, their spirits flow,
As they journey beneath heavens above.

Through storms and calm, they shall remain,
Two souls united in joy and pain.

The Quietude of Us

In soft whispers, our hearts align,
A world created with just a sigh.
Moments linger, pure and divine,
In the stillness, we learn to fly.

The silence speaks in gentle tones,
Where words are few, yet meanings swell.
Our laughter dances through the bones,
In this quietude, love's sweet spell.

Each heartbeat echoes a calming tune,
A lullaby wrapped in embrace.
Beneath the watchful gaze of the moon,
We chart our dreams in sacred space.

In every pause, our spirits blend,
As time slips softly into night.
Together bound, we'll never end,
In this quietude, everything feels right.

Hand in hand, through dusk and dawn,
Our love is a quiet serenade.

A Sanctuary of Two

In a quiet hideaway, we find,
A sanctuary meant for just us.
With every moment, our hearts unwind,
Creating memories we can trust.

Walls adorned with laughter bright,
Echoes of joy, a soothing balm.
In our fortress, passion ignites,
Wrapping us in a sacred calm.

Windows open to the world so wide,
Yet here we dwell in our own dream.
With love as a guide, we gently stride,
Together flowing like a stream.

Through every season, we will grow,
In the beauty of our shared embrace.
A sanctuary only we know,
A haven, our sacred place.

Together we paint our skies anew,
In this sanctuary meant for two.

Laughter in Echoing Chambers

In the halls where laughter swells,
Echoes dance with joyous glee.
Every corner softly tells,
Of moments shared, just you and me.

The music of our playful hearts,
Resonating through the air.
In different notes, our love imparts,
A melody that's bright and rare.

We spin in circles, hand in hand,
Creating ripples, bright and bold.
In this joy, we take a stand,
As laughter's warmth begins to unfold.

In chambers filled with pure delight,
We craft a world, our own refrain.
Through the echoes, day and night,
Our laughter lingers, free from pain.

With every giggle, every cheer,
We write a story, blissfully clear.

Starlit Conversations

On a blanket beneath the sky,
Whispers of secrets pass by.
Stars twinkle with soft delight,
In the warmth of the night.

Moonlight dances on your face,
In this serene, sacred space.
Words flow like a gentle stream,
A tapestry of our dream.

The night hums a lullaby,
While the world seems to sigh.
Each glance, a silent vow,
In this moment, here and now.

Time stands still, we're intertwined,
In the echo of hearts aligned.
Each heartbeat a gentle sign,
In starlit conversations, you're mine.

Under the cosmos, secrets thrive,
In this space, our love's alive.
The universe, a witness true,
As I hold the stars with you.

Synchronized Dreams

In the twilight where shadows meet,
We drift as time has no seat.
With our hearts, we paint the skies,
Breathing life into our sighs.

Every wish, a shared delight,
In the quiet of the night.
Your laughter, a melody sweet,
In my dreams, our souls repeat.

Guided by stars, we explore,
With each secret, we want more.
Hand in hand, we chase the dawn,
In synchronized dreams, we're drawn.

Through the fabric of the night,
We weave futures, pure and bright.
As we dance on this soft stream,
Life is perfect in our dream.

With each moment, we transcend,
A tale of love with no end.
In the hush, our hearts unite,
In synchronized dreams, our flight.

Echoes of Affection

In the stillness, hearts converse,
Every heartbeat, a soft verse.
In the shadows, tender grace,
You're the light I want to chase.

Our laughter plays a sweet refrain,
Echoes of love dance in the rain.
With every touch and every sigh,
A whisper travels, soaring high.

Through the moments, shared and new,
The echoes bring me back to you.
In your gaze, my worries cease,
In your arms, I find my peace.

Letters written in the stars,
Our story told, no more scars.
Each memory a precious song,
In the echoes, we belong.

As the night plays its sweet tune,
Underneath the watchful moon.
We linger in the tender light,
In echoes of affection, so right.

The Dance of Us

Two souls meet on the floor,
In the rhythm, we explore.
With each beat, we learn to sway,
In the dance, we find our way.

Every step feels like a dream,
In this moment, hearts redeem.
With your smile guiding me near,
All my doubts disappear.

We twirl beneath the endless sky,
In each gaze, we silently fly.
With laughter echoing our sway,
The dance of us lights the way.

Together, we spin and glide,
In this rhythm, love's our guide.
The world fades, it's just we two,
In the dance, I'm lost in you.

With each turn, we weave our fate,
As the night begins to wait.
Under stars, our spirits soar,
In the dance of us, forevermore.

Threads of Destiny

In the fabric of time, we weave,
With threads of fate, we believe.
Stitching dreams, oh so bright,
Guided by stars in the night.

Paths cross in the silent air,
A moment shared, a gentle care.
Each knot a promise softly made,
In the tapestry, our fears fade.

Woven tightly, we stand strong,
In the chorus of our song.
The colors blend, the patterns glow,
Together we rise, destined to grow.

Every stitch a tale to tell,
Of love that blooms where shadows fell.
In this design, our hearts align,
Threads of destiny, forever divine.

The Bond Beyond Words

In quiet moments, we find grace,
A look exchanged, no need to chase.
In silence deep, our hearts can speak,
A language formed in every peek.

Through laughter shared and tears we shed,
In tender glances, love is fed.
A bond unseen, yet strong and true,
In every thought, I'm bound to you.

When storms arise and shadows creep,
Your hand in mine, my heart can leap.
A fortress built on trust and care,
In this embrace, we're always there.

Words may falter, but we shall not,
In every silence, love hits the spot.
The bond we share, a sacred thread,
Beyond what's spoken, deeply spread.

Orbiting Each Other

Like planets in a dance so grand,
We move in sync, hand in hand.
Our paths aligned, a cosmic flow,
In this vast space, our love will grow.

You are the sun, I am the moon,
In your light, I find my tune.
Circling close, yet free to roam,
Together we build our shared home.

Gravity pulls, a force so pure,
In every heartbeat, we endure.
Around and around, we spin with grace,
In the universe, we've found our place.

Through every rise, through every fall,
We orbit close, answering the call.
In this celestial dance, we find our way,
Orbiting each other, day to day.

Hearts Entwined in Rhythm

In the beat of time, we sway,
With every note, we find our way.
Jazz and blues in whispered tones,
Our hearts entwined, no need for loans.

In harmony, we laugh and play,
Each moment cherished, come what may.
With every glance, a spark ignites,
A symphony that feels so right.

Through highs and lows, we dance along,
In the silence, you hear our song.
A melody that never ends,
Together always, love transcends.

With every step, our souls align,
In this rhythm, your heart is mine.
Entwined in love, we find our beat,
Hearts in sync, a bond so sweet.

Labyrinth of Affection

In the maze where hearts entwine,
Whispers echo, souls align.
Every turn reveals a clue,
In this dance, just me and you.

Through the twists and tangled bends,
Love's warm light never ends.
Hand in hand, we brave the night,
Together, we find the light.

Hurdles rise, yet we stay true,
In the depths, we always knew.
Lost within these paths so wide,
In each other, we confide.

Moments drip like candle wax,
Softly binding all our tracks.
In this puzzle, we create,
A haven we cultivate.

Through the shadows, joy will gleam,
In this labyrinth, we dream.
Two hearts charting every way,
Finding peace in love's ballet.

A Canvas of Togetherness

Brush strokes dance on our shared space,
Colors blend in a warm embrace.
Every hue tells our own tale,
On this canvas, love won't fail.

With laughter as our brightest shade,
Joyful moments never fade.
In every corner, memories bloom,
Painting life in every room.

Whispers wrapped in calm delight,
Together, we ignite the night.
Strokes of trust, so bold and bright,
Layered dreams in morning light.

Each moment, a brush that swirls,
Creating magic in our worlds.
With every heartbeat, art unfolds,
In our hands, a story told.

Underneath a sky so vast,
Embracing now, forgetting past.
A masterpiece that's yet to be,
In this journey, you and me.

Whirls of Emotion

Spinning round, I feel the spark,
Your laughter lights up the dark.
In this whirl, we lose the day,
Caught in joy, we drift away.

Each tear is a glimmer, a sigh,
In the tempest, we learn to fly.
Through the storm, together we sway,
Holding tight, come what may.

Passions rise like autumn leaves,
In this dance, our heart believes.
Every turn, a whisper sweet,
In this rhythm, we compete.

Moments twirl as shadows blend,
In this vortex, love won't end.
With every spin, the world grows bright,
In your arms, I find my light.

Through the whirls of sweet embrace,
Time stands still in this sacred space.
Forever lost in this delight,
Together we paint the night.

The Warmth Between Us

In the quiet glow, we find our peace,
With gentle hands, the world's release,
A warmth that brews in every touch,
In the warmth between us, means so much.

Underneath the starry skies,
In whispered dreams, our love complies,
An ember glows, igniting fire,
In the warmth between us, heart's desire.

A soothing balm, our laughter plays,
In simple moments, love conveys,
With every glance, a spark ignites,
In the warmth between us, pure delights.

Through seasons change, our bond will stay,
Like golden rays at close of day,
Together we thrive, rising high,
In the warmth between us, we can fly.

So hold me close, let hearts entwine,
Through all the storms, your hand in mine,
For in this love, we find the way,
In the warmth between us, come what may.

A Symphony of Union

In harmony, our hearts align,
A melody that feels divine,
With every note, our spirits rise,
In a symphony, love never dies.

Together, we weave our song,
Each gentle chord, where we belong,
Through trials faced, we find the way,
A symphony that's here to stay.

With every breath, we find the tune,
A dance beneath the silvery moon,
As laughter mingles with each sigh,
In a symphony, love won't die.

Our voices blend like sweet perfume,
In every echo, there's room to bloom,
A world created, just for us,
A symphony of timeless trust.

So let the music fill the air,
With every beat, our souls laid bare,
In joyous rhythm, we unite,
A symphony, our hearts ignite.

Moonlit promises

Beneath the silver glow, we tread,
A quiet place where dreams are fed,
Whispers dance on the evening air,
In moonlit promises, we share.

Stars above like lanterns bright,
Guide our hearts through the endless night,
With every step, our spirits soar,
In this moment, we seek no more.

The world fades, it's just us two,
In shadows deep, our love is true,
Caught in the spell of night's embrace,
In moonlit promises, we find grace.

Each heartbeat sings a sweet refrain,
Of hopes renewed and past refrain,
Together we chase tomorrow's light,
As promises gleam in the soft twilight.

So let the night hold our secrets dear,
In its stillness, our path is clear,
With faith ablaze, we will abide,
In moonlit promises, side by side.

Beneath Our Veil

Softly woven, threads of fate,
Underneath this woven state.
Under stars, our spirits twine,
Beneath this veil, your heart is mine.

Gentle whispers, secrets shared,
In this realm, we both declared.
With our dreams as our escape,
In this cover, we reshape.

Shadows dance behind the light,
Every breath feels just so right.
Hands entwined in purest grace,
In our world, we've found our place.

Underneath our soft disguise,
Love awakens, never lies.
In this haven, hope prevails,
Together, we lift the veils.

As the moon sings lullabies,
We embark on sweet goodbyes.
Yet in dreams, we shall unite,
Beneath the veil, love ignites.

Portraits of Affection

In every glance, a story told,
Of whispered dreams and hearts of gold,
Each brushstroke deep, a vibrant hue,
In portraits of affection, me and you.

Captured moments, time stands still,
Faces glow with a tender thrill,
Love paints our lives with shades unique,
In portraits of affection, love's mystique.

Through laughter's shine and sorrow's tear,
Each moment shared, we hold so dear,
A canvas bright, our spirits blend,
In portraits of affection, hearts transcend.

Reflections dance in twilight's light,
As we embrace the falling night,
Together framed, we take our stance,
In portraits of affection, love's romance.

So let us pause, and gaze awhile,
At every joy, a fleeting smile,
For in this gallery, love shines through,
In portraits of affection, me and you.

Secrets in the Shadows

Whispers weave through the night air,
Hidden truths with quiet care.
Moonlight dances on silent dreams,
Fractured hopes, or so it seems.

A rustle here, a sigh over there,
Secrets linger, a delicate snare.
Behind closed doors, shadows play,
Veiling words we dare not say.

In corners dim, hidden hearts beat,
Gathering stories where night and day meet.
Every glance, a tale untold,
In shadows deep, the brave grow bold.

Threads of silence intertwined,
Each secret shared, a heart aligned.
In the darkness, a bond is sewn,
In whispered tones, we find our own.

Secrets thrive where light feels scarce,
In the hush, there lies a fierce embrace.
Beneath the stars, our fears subside,
In shadows deep, love's truth will bide.

Love's Unspoken Language

In a glance, a world unfolds,
Silent stories, shyly told.
The touch of hands, a fleeting spark,
Words unsaid, yet lighting dark.

In the stillness, hearts shall dance,
Captured in a whispered chance.
Every heartbeat, a secret song,
In love's embrace, we both belong.

Lingering sighs and breaths aligned,
In the silence, our souls entwined.
A smile shared, a moment clear,
In each glance, the love draws near.

Unfolding feelings, night and day,
In soft shadows, we find our way.
With every pause, we find the right,
Love blooms bright against the night.

In the space between, we find the grace,
A language spoken in a trace.
In its rhythm, magic we find,
Love's unspoken, forever kind.

In the Heart's Assembly

Gathered close in fellowship tight,
Hearts convene in soft twilight.
Emotions shared like gentle rain,
Binding souls with joy and pain.

Every rhythm, a likeness found,
Within this circle, love abounds.
Laughter dances, shadows lift,
In unity, our greatest gift.

Unraveled hopes upon the floor,
Together we rise, we learn, explore.
With every story, our worlds collide,
In the heart's assembly, love won't hide.

As tears may fall, they strengthen ties,
In the silence, understanding lies.
Gathered souls, woven seams,
In every heartbeat, we share dreams.

Against the odds, we find our way,
In unity, come what may.
Each bond a treasure, dear and bright,
In the heart's assembly, love ignites.

Echoes of Affection

In the quiet, whispers blend,
Every heartbeat, a gentle friend.
Echoes linger, soft and sweet,
In the silence, our rhythms meet.

Memories carved in time's embrace,
Every glance, a tender trace.
Your laughter dances on the breeze,
In every moment, love's sweet tease.

Silent promises in the night,
Wrapped in dreams, we take our flight.
With every step, the echoes grow,
In each caress, the love we show.

Voices soft like fading light,
In the darkness, hearts unite.
Every whisper, a sacred vow,
In echoes deep, we find our now.

With every heartbeat, we remain,
In echoes pure, love cannot wane.
In the quiet, a bond we find,
Echoes of affection, forever entwined.

The Language of Heartstrings

In whispers soft, our hearts align,
A rhythm found, a dance divine.
Beneath the stars, our secrets shared,
In silent poses, love declared.

With every glance, a story told,
Of dreams once bright, now manifold.
The touch of hands, a spark ignites,
Creating warmth on winter nights.

In laughter bold, our spirits soar,
A symphony beyond decor.
Through gentle sighs and knowing smiles,
We bridge the gaps of endless miles.

Through trials faced, we rise anew,
With courage born from love so true.
In every heartbeat, echoes rhyme,
A melody defying time.

So let us dance in twilight's glow,
In the embrace of love we know.
For in this life of ebb and flow,
Our heartstrings weave, forever grow.

Timeless Expressions

In fleeting moments, time stands still,
A canvas stretched by fate's own will.
With every glance, a picture drawn,
Of laughter shared with each new dawn.

Our words are soft, like gentle rain,
Each drop a soothing balm for pain.
Across the years, memories flow,
In timeless expressions, love will grow.

Through seasons change, we find our way,
In sunlit blooms of bright array.
An artful glance, a tender kiss,
Each cherished moment, purest bliss.

The echoes of our laughter ring,
In symphonies that hope can bring.
With every heartbeat, truths we show,
In timeless expressions, love will grow.

In twilight's hue, we dance and sway,
With every breath, we find our play.
For love is art, forever new,
An endless canvas, me and you.

Mirth of Two Souls

In laughter shared, our spirit gleams,
Two souls entwined in woven dreams.
With playful jests, the world recedes,
Fueling the light from simple deeds.

In secrets kept and stories spun,
Through every challenge, laughter won.
A gentle nudge, a knowing glance,
In the sweet rhythm of our dance.

In twilight's hush, we chase the stars,
With joyous hearts, we heal our scars.
The mirth we share, an endless stream,
Imbued with love, a vibrant theme.

Through paths we tread, both rough and bright,
The mirth we share ignites the night.
In every laugh, a promise made,
Together in this grand charade.

So here we stand, two hearts a-whirl,
In the sweet joy of life's unfurl.
For in this laughter, bright and true,
Lies the deep bond of me and you.

Threads of Intimacy

In gentle threads, our lives entwine,
Woven in moments, pure and fine.
With every breath, a bond we weave,
In the tapestry of love, believe.

Through shared glances, soft and deep,
In secrets guarded, hearts we keep.
With whispers light, like morning dew,
The threads of us are strong and true.

In twilight's glow, together stand,
With open hearts and joined hands.
Through trials faced and joy embraced,
In every moment, love interlaced.

As time moves on, our paths will bend,
But in this bond, we find our blend.
For in the quiet, in the storm,
These threads of intimacy keep us warm.

So let us cherish, day by day,
The woven threads that guide our way.
In the dance of life, just me and you,
Forever stitched with love anew.

Enchanted Encounters

In twilight's glow, we softly tread,
Two souls adrift, where dreams are fed.
Through whispered winds and rustling leaves,
Magic lingers, as the heart believes.

With every glance, a spark ignites,
In the hush of night, beneath the lights.
A dance of fate, where shadows play,
Enchanted moments guide our way.

The stars above, our silent cheer,
In this embrace, we conquer fear.
Eyes entwined, secrets unfold,
In this story, love turns bold.

Beneath the moon, we find our song,
A melody where we belong.
Through laughter, joy, and gentle sighs,
In every meeting, a sweet surprise.

As dawn breaks forth, we'll hold on tight,
To fleeting dreams that take their flight.
In enchanted moments, we will find,
The depth of love that ties the mind.

Veils of Understanding

In silence shared, a truth revealed,
Two heartbeats merge, the pain healed.
Through veils of doubt, we seek the light,
Navigating depths, embracing the night.

With whispered words that softly flow,
Each layer peeled, the juices sow.
A tapestry woven, thread by thread,
Binding our stories; love is fed.

In gentle glances, meaning lingers,
Each touch ignites, like dancing fingers.
Beneath the surface, layers untwine,
In veils of time, our souls align.

Through storms and calm, we bravely stand,
Unraveling mysteries hand in hand.
In every challenge, we find our grace,
With open hearts, we embrace our place.

In sacred trust, a bond defined,
With every moment, love intertwined.
Veils of understanding softly part,
Revealing the depths of a tender heart.

Journey Beyond Words

In realms of thought where silence speaks,
A journey starts, the spirit seeks.
Through winding paths and whispered dreams,
Beyond the words, the heart redeems.

With open eyes, we traverse the grey,
Exploring shadows that dance and play.
In every pause, a story sways,
Journeying deep through uncharted ways.

The language of souls, no need for sound,
In shared breaths, our truth is found.
With each heartbeat, bridges span,
A cosmic dance, both woman and man.

In sacred spaces, where silence glow,
Peering deeper, we come to know.
Beyond the cliffs, where thoughts unfurl,
In this journey, we embrace the world.

With every step, a lesson marked,
In the quiet places where love sparked.
Our journey flows, no end in sight,
Beyond the words, we find our light.

In the Realm of Us

In the realm of us, where dreams reside,
Two hearts converge, on love's great tide.
With whispered truths and laughter bright,
We carve our path, igniting light.

Through seasons change, and time unfolds,
Every moment, a tale retold.
In the snapshots of a shared embrace,
We find our rhythm, a sacred space.

In silence deep, we understand,
A connection forged, unbreakable strand.
With every glance, the world aligns,
In the realm of us, the heart defines.

Each challenge met, we rise anew,
With strength found in the bond we grew.
In love's embrace, the fabric we weave,
United, we dream, together believe.

As stars align in endless dance,
In the realm of us, we take a chance.
With hope in hand, and dreams in sight,
Together we soar, into the night.

Journeys of Together

Hand in hand, we walk the road,
Through sunlit paths and heavy load.
Each step a story yet untold,
In laughter's warmth, our hearts unfold.

With every turn, new sights to see,
The world unfolds, just you and me.
In whispered dreams, our hopes align,
In every moment, love's design.

The mountains rise, the rivers flow,
In every heartbeat, love will grow.
Together strong, we face the fight,
Our souls entwined, a radiant light.

Through storms that rage and clouds that cry,
We find our peace beneath the sky.
In every challenge, hand held tight,
Our bond, a beacon in the night.

So here's to journeys far and near,
In every laugh, we hold dear.
As time unfolds, we'll walk as one,
Our journey's joy has just begun.

Tapestry of Tenderness

In threads of gold, our stories weave,
Each moment shared, a heart we believe.
Colors blend in soft embrace,
A tapestry of love and grace.

With gentle hands, we stitch our dreams,
In quiet whispers, our laughter gleams.
Embracing flaws, we find our way,
In every heartbeat, come what may.

The fabric strong, the patterns bright,
In darkened days, we find our light.
Together we can mend the seams,
In fragile nights, we share our dreams.

As seasons shift and time does flow,
Our tapestry will ever grow.
In every patch, a love that's true,
A masterpiece crafted by me and you.

So let us weave with threads divine,
In every stitch, our hearts entwine.
For in this art, we both shall find,
A tapestry of hearts aligned.

Love's Shared Reverie

Beneath the stars, two souls will meet,
In every glance, a spark, a heat.
We dance in shadows, lost in time,
In whispered verses, love's sweet rhyme.

With every dream, we take our flight,
Through moonlit paths, a shared delight.
In gentle sighs, our secrets trace,
Together lost in love's embrace.

Through every tear and joyful cry,
We paint our world, you and I.
In painted skies our hopes extend,
In love's embrace, our hearts will mend.

The echoes of our laughter blend,
In cherished moments, we transcend.
Each heartbeat claims this vivid art,
In love's shared reverie, we start.

So hold me close, don't let me go,
In this sweet dance, let our love grow.
For in the dreams that we create,
Is where our hearts will find their fate.

In the Circle of Trust

A sacred space where spirits meet,
Within this circle, love's heartbeat.
In laughter's glow and whispers low,
We build a bond that only we know.

With open hearts, we share our fears,
In every joy, in every tear.
Holding hands, our spirits lift,
In the circle, a cherished gift.

Through winds of change and tides so strong,
We find our place, where we belong.
In unity, our roots run deep,
In this embrace, our promises keep.

In shadows dark, we stand as one,
Through battles lost, and victories won.
In trust we find a light so bright,
A guiding star that shines each night.

So let us gather, side by side,
In the circle of trust, our hearts abide.
Together we shall face the dawn,
In love's embrace, forever drawn.

The Beauty of Coexistence

In a garden where all bloom,
Colors blend and dispel gloom,
Bees and flowers share their song,
In harmony, they all belong.

Different voices, all unique,
Every creature, every peak,
Together in this vibrant place,
Unity fills the space.

Mountains rise, rivers flow,
A tapestry of life we sow,
In the air, a gentle breeze,
We embrace, we find our ease.

From the skies to ocean's depths,
Each life thrives, none are left,
In this dance, we intertwine,
Life's a gift, a grand design.

Let us cherish what we share,
In this world, with love and care,
For in diversity's embrace,
Lies the beauty of our grace.

Kaleidoscope of Love

Colors swirl, they intertwine,
Every shade, a heart's design,
In your eyes, the world unfolds,
A love story forever told.

From the dawn to twilight's chime,
Every moment, pure and sublime,
A dance of hearts, a soft embrace,
In this kaleidoscope, we trace.

Fragments bright from days gone by,
Whispers, laughter, dreams that fly,
In the tapestry, we find our song,
With every note, we both belong.

As the moonlight softly glows,
In your warmth, my spirit knows,
Together, we create and mend,
In this wonder, love won't end.

Through the seasons, hand in hand,
In each heartbeat, a promise stands,
An endless spiral, ever true,
My kaleidoscope is you.

Wishes Beneath the Stars

Gazing upward, dreams take flight,
Wishes whispered into night,
Each twinkle holds a silent prayer,
In the cosmos, hopes laid bare.

Stardust dances in the skies,
Filling hearts with sweet sighs,
With each flicker, a story spins,
Of where hope begins and wins.

Underneath the velvet dark,
We share our dreams, we leave a mark,
In the stillness, the world aligns,
In quiet moments, love defines.

As constellations weave their fate,
In the glow, we patiently wait,
For every wish the heavens grant,
In the silence, our hearts chant.

United by the countless lights,
In their glow, our future bright,
With every star, a journey starts,
Wishes shared, entwined our hearts.

Enigmas of Affection

In every glance, a mystery,
A riddle wrapped in history,
Through whispered words, secrets spin,
In this dance, where we begin.

Soft touch, electric charge,
Emotions rise and sometimes enlarge,
In the silence, loud we feel,
A puzzle of hearts, perfectly real.

From laughter's echo to tears' rain,
In every joy, in every pain,
We navigate this wondrous maze,
Finding love in all its ways.

Hidden meanings in your smile,
Each moment gives, each moment's trial,
With every heartbeat, truths revealed,
In affection, our souls are healed.

Forever chasing the unknown,
In this labyrinth, we'll have grown,
Embracing all the paths we tread,
In enigmas, our love is bred.

Whispers in the Twilight

Soft shadows dance at night,
As stars begin to glow bright.
The moon whispers secrets low,
In this gentle twilight flow.

Breezes carry silent dreams,
As time weaves its silver seams.
Crickets sing in quiet cheer,
Embracing peace, holding near.

Glimmers flicker through the trees,
Awakening the evening breeze.
Each whisper stirs the heart's flame,
Enchanting every soul's name.

Darkness cloaks the world in grace,
In solitude, we find our place.
With every breath, we feel alive,
In twilight's arms, we gently thrive.

The night unveils its tender art,
Binding every wandering heart.
Together here, we find our way,
In whispered dreams where shadows play.

Together in Reverie

In dreams we walk, hand in hand,
Creating worlds, a vibrant land.
With every step, our spirits soar,
In realms of magic, we explore.

You and I in harmony,
Crafting tales, just you and me.
Time dissolves, we laugh and sing,
In this moment, joy takes wing.

The colors burst, so vivid, bright,
Painting our hearts in pure delight.
Whispers of love fill the air,
Together here, we have no care.

A gentle breeze caresses skin,
In this reverie, where love begins.
No fears remain; we are set free,
In our dreams, just you and me.

As dawn approaches, light will break,
But in our hearts, this dream won't shake.
Together in reverie we stand,
A timeless bond, forever planned.

Harmonies of Heartbeat

In the silence, hearts align,
Beating softly, yours and mine.
Rhythms blend, a sacred song,
In this embrace, we both belong.

Moments weave in sweet refrain,
Echoes dance like softest rain.
With each thump, our souls ignite,
Harmonies in the still of night.

Whispers linger where we meet,
Tension fades with every beat.
In the cadence of our truth,
Love resounds, eternal proof.

Let the world fade far away,
In our hearts, forever stay.
With each breath, we intertwine,
In this melody, love divine.

Together in this symphony,
Finding solace, pure and free.
Harmonies swell, a timeless art,
Forever bound, heart to heart.

Embracing the Unseen

In shadows cast by light's retreat,
Lies beauty wrapped in quiet heat.
The unseen whispers tales untold,
In gentle hands, our dreams unfold.

Mysteries dance just out of sight,
Guiding us through the still of night.
Embracing all that hides away,
In the dark, we find our play.

Moments spark in veils of gray,
Illuminating our hidden way.
With every breath, the path reveals,
Strength in silence, love that heals.

Though unseen, our spirits soar,
Through every opening, every door.
In shadows where our hearts have been,
We rise to greet the world unseen.

Together in this quiet place,
We find our truth, our sacred space.
Embracing all that lies between,
In the depths, we live serene.

The Symphony of Togetherness

In harmony we stand, side by side,
Each note a promise, a love we can't hide.
In laughter, in silence, we find our song,
Together we flourish, where we both belong.

With every heartbeat, a rhythm we weave,
A tapestry rich, in what we believe.
Through trials and joy, we dance in the light,
Together, our symphony feels so right.

In moments of stillness, our souls align,
The beauty of union, like vintage wine.
With every embrace, a melody clear,
In the symphony of us, there's nothing to fear.

Love's Gentle Cadence

In whispers and glances, our feelings unfold,
A rhythm of love, a story retold.
In tender embraces, we find our way,
With each gentle heartbeat, come what may.

Through sunlit mornings and moonlit nights,
Our hearts play a tune, in soft, sweet delights.
With laughter that dances like fireflies' glow,
In love's gentle cadence, we flourish and grow.

In the stillness of moments, our spirits entwine,
A melody captured, ineffably divine.
With every sweet sigh, our souls intertwine,
In love's gentle cadence, forever, you're mine.

Across a Shared Horizon

Together we stand, on the edge of the day,
Chasing the colors as they fade away.
With hands intertwined, we venture afar,
Across a shared horizon, guided by stars.

In twilight's embrace, our dreams dance and play,
Each whisper, a promise, to never stray.
Through valleys and peaks, our spirits ascend,
With love as our compass, on each other depend.

As dawn stretches gold, igniting the morn,
We greet every challenge, reborn and adorned.
With hearts wide as oceans, we see life unfold,
Across a shared horizon, our story is told.

Shadows of Kinship

In the depth of silence, kinship does bloom,
Casting gentle shadows that light up the room.
Through laughter and tears, we journey as one,
In the shadows of kinship, our hearts are spun.

With every shared glance, our warmth is revealed,
The strength of our bond, a treasure concealed.
In moments of sorrow, we stand hand in hand,
Together we weather, together we stand.

In stories exchanged, our histories blend,
With love in our hearts, on each other we depend.
In shadows of kinship, forever we'll stay,
A tapestry woven, in colors that play.

Paths Merging in Harmony

Two roads converge with gentle grace,
Soft whispers linger in this place.
Hearts align, a shared refrain,
Under the sky, we break the chain.

Footsteps blend on this winding way,
Guided by love, come what may.
In every turn, trust will unfold,
Together we forge, brave and bold.

Each moment blooms where wishes meet,
In harmony, our souls complete.
Through storms and sun, we carry on,
In the dance of life, our bond is strong.

With every breath, we write our song,
In unity, we both belong.
Paths merge, creating a new name,
In love's embrace, we fan the flame.

Cradle of Affection

In gentle arms, the world feels right,
Softly cradled, hearts take flight.
With tender thoughts that softly weave,
A tapestry that we believe.

Every glance, a loving touch,
In this cradle, we feel so much.
The warmth of you, my guiding star,
In the quiet night, you're never far.

Time stands still, a sacred space,
Fingers entwined, we find our pace.
Each heartbeat echoes sweet and clear,
In the cradle of love, we find no fear.

With dreams like whispers in the air,
A silent promise, always there.
In this embrace, forever stay,
In a cradle forged from yesterday.

Tides of Togetherness

Waves cascade with gentle might,
Together we stand, hearts so light.
As tides rise high, we ebb and flow,
In harmony's grasp, our love will grow.

Every ripple, a shared delight,
In the shadows, we find our light.
With hands held tight, we face the sea,
In the tides of life, there's you and me.

The horizon calls with whispers sweet,
Every journey, our hearts repeat.
On this shore, we greet the dawn,
In the dance of waves, we are reborn.

Bound together through storm and strife,
In every wave, we find our life.
Tides of togetherness softly hum,
In love's embrace, we are always one.

Chasing the Horizon Hand in Hand

With every step, we seek the bright,
Chasing horizons bathed in light.
Hand in hand, we rise and soar,
Through fields of dreams, forevermore.

The dawn is painted in hues of hope,
Together we climb, learn to cope.
With laughter spanning every mile,
In each glance, we share a smile.

As shadows stretch and evening falls,
In whispered words, our love calls.
Across the sunset, we boldly roam,
In every heartbeat, we find our home.

In the vastness where dreams expand,
We chase the horizon, united we stand.
With courage woven into our plan,
Hand in hand, we'll always span.

Moments Suspended

In the stillness of the night,
Stars whisper secrets bright,
Time slows to catch a breath,
Life dances on the edge of death.

Captured thoughts like fleeting dreams,
Glowing softly in moonbeams,
Each second holds a world,
In silence, our hearts unfurled.

With each heartbeat, threads unite,
Weaving tales in twilight's light,
Emotions drift like softest snow,
In this moment, we truly know.

As shadows blend and fade away,
Hope emerges at break of day,
In suspension, we find grace,
Time and love, a warm embrace.

Breathe in deep the gentle night,
Moments paused, pure delight,
With open hearts, we stand as one,
In life's embrace, we're never done.

Reflections of Us

In mirrors clear, our faces shine,
Every smile, a sacred sign,
Through laughter's ring and whispers near,
Love's reflection is crystal clear.

With every glance, a story told,
Pages turning, hearts unfold,
In shadows cast, we find our way,
Together, in the light of day.

Fragmented dreams, like shattered glass,
We piece together as we pass,
In silent rooms and crowded streets,
Our essence found in heartbeats.

Threads of fate, woven tight,
In chaos, we ignite the light,
Reflections dance, together we sway,
Even as the world slips away.

Glimmers of truth in every glance,
With courage, we take the chance,
To see ourselves in love's embrace,
Reflections of us, a timeless space.

Kin in Quietude

Amidst the noise, we find our peace,
In whispered thoughts, our worries cease,
Connected threads in silence weave,
In quietude, we learn to believe.

Gentle breezes wrap around,
Nature's calm, a soothing sound,
With every breath, a bond is formed,
In stillness, we are forever warmed.

Eyes meet in the softest glow,
Sharing secrets only we know,
In the hush, our spirits soar,
Like waves that kiss the quiet shore.

Understanding blooms in calmness rare,
In tranquil moments, love lays bare,
Together, we walk a path of grace,
Kin in quietude, our sacred space.

Here in the still, we find our might,
With gentle hearts, we embrace the night,
Roots entwined in earth's soft hand,
In quietude, together we stand.

Connected in Chaos

In the whirlwind, we find our voice,
Dancing among the chaos, we choice,
Amidst the storm, we grasp the hand,
Together, we bravely make our stand.

Fractured worlds, we hold them tight,
In the darkest hours, we ignite the light,
Each voice a color, each heart a song,
In harmony, we right the wrong.

Through tangled paths and frantic beats,
We seek the calm in bustling streets,
Interwoven dreams in every glance,
Connected souls in life's wild dance.

As tempests roar and shadows grow,
We find the strength in what we know,
In chaos, we create a spark,
Guiding each other through the dark.

Hand in hand, through thick and thin,
In the chaos, where love begins,
Together forever, we rise above,
Connected in chaos, bound by love.

Secrets Beneath the Stars

In whispered night, the sky unfolds,
Stories of dreams, and fables old.
Each star a secret, a tale to tell,
In shadows deep, where wonders dwell.

Moonlight kisses the restless sea,
Echoes of whispers set the mind free.
In silence vast, hearts intertwine,
Beneath the stars, our souls align.

Comets blaze with fleeting grace,
Carving paths in the timeless space.
In their wake, our wishes soar,
To distant realms, forevermore.

Eclipses cloak the hidden truth,
Veils of night reveal our youth.
With every twinkle, a promise made,
In cosmic light, our fears will fade.

So let us wander, hand in hand,
Through fields of dreams, in stardust land.
The universe whispers, a secret tune,
Together we dance, beneath the moon.

Unity in Solitude

In quiet moments, we find our peace,
The world fades, and troubles cease.
Within ourselves, a spark ignites,
In solitude, our spirit writes.

Wandering paths of thought replete,
We find the rhythm, a gentle beat.
In shadows cast by silent nights,
Our inner strength, a guiding light.

Breathing deep the stillness near,
We learn to face our hidden fear.
Each heartbeat echoes, strong and true,
In solitude, we are renewed.

Alone we stand, yet never lost,
In self-reflection, we bear the cost.
Embracing whispers of the mind,
In unity, our souls aligned.

Through winds of change, we stand so bold,
In our hearts, a warmth to hold.
For in each moment, silent, pure,
We find the strength to endure.

So cherish time, in stillness found,
For in this realm, our hearts are bound.
Amidst the chaos, let us see,
In solitude, we're truly free.

Tapestry of Two

Woven threads of different hues,
Tie our hearts, as love renews.
Each moment stitched with care and grace,
In this tapestry, we find our place.

Patterns formed in laughter bright,
Shared secrets dance in the soft moonlight.
In every thread, a story spun,
Together we rise, we've just begun.

The fabric strong, yet delicate too,
Our bond is fierce, ever true.
With stitches tight, we weather storms,
In each embrace, our spirit warms.

Colors blend, in perfect array,
Hand in hand, we find our way.
Each challenge faced, a lesson learned,
In this weave of love, we are returned.

With every knot, a promise made,
In this art, we are not afraid.
For in the weave, our souls reside,
A tapestry of two, side by side.

So let us cherish this design so rare,
In life's grand loom, a love to share.
Together we'll weave, the stories unfold,
In the tapestry of us, our hearts are bold.

Interwoven Journeys

Paths may cross, or drift apart,
Yet every step, a work of art.
In journeys taken, lessons found,
In shared experiences, we're profound.

Footprints linger on the shore,
Marking times we can't ignore.
In laughter shared, or tears that fall,
We rise and stumble, through it all.

Together we wander through life's grand maze,
Each twist and turn, a vibrant phase.
In moments fleeting, memories cling,
As time unveils what love can bring.

From sunrise hues to twilight's glow,
In every heartbeat, our spirits grow.
Through trials faced and joys embraced,
In this journey, we're interlaced.

As seasons change and rivers flow,
Our paths may part, yet still, we know.
In each adventure, a bond remains,
Interwoven souls, through joy and pains.

So here's to the travels, both near and far,
In every journey, we raise the bar.
For as we wander, our hearts inspired,
In union, we thrive, forever wired.

A Bridge of Understanding

Across the river, dreams unfold,
Whispers of hope in stories told.
Hearts open wide, in gentle grace,
Finding the strength in a shared place.

Steps we take, hand in hand,
Building a pathway, across the land.
Kindred spirits share their truth,
In the embrace of our common youth.

Voices rise, a melodic tune,
Under the watch of the kind moon.
Listening close, we bridge the divide,
Connecting our souls, with love as our guide.

Every laugh, every tear we share,
Threads of compassion, woven with care.
No more silence, let our hearts sing,
In this unity, together we bring.

In the quiet, understanding grows,
Nurtured by peace, where kindness flows.
Together we rise, stronger than before,
A bridge of understanding forevermore.

Unity in Diversity

Colors blend in the grand parade,
Every hue a story made.
Different voices, a single song,
In this chorus, we all belong.

Hands of many, clasped in grace,
United we stand, in this shared space.
Each unique thread in our vast weave,
In diversity's strength, we believe.

Cultures dance under the same sky,
Harmony rising, a hopeful sigh.
Different paths, but one goal in sight,
Together we walk, igniting the light.

Embracing the tales that we bear,
Learning from love, and showing we care.
In differences, beauty shall thrive,
Unity found, we come alive.

Let empathy guide every stride,
In the fabric of life, we find our pride.
Together we dream, together we sing,
In the heart of humanity, our future takes wing.

Unveiling the Bonds

In every smile, connection blooms,
Familiar whispers fill the rooms.
Stories woven, destinies shared,
In the tapestry of hearts, we dared.

Veils of silence fall away,
Bringing forth light into the day.
Through laughter and tears, we unveil,
These bonds of love that shall not pale.

Moments captured, memories made,
In the warmth of kindness, fear will fade.
Holding each other in the storm,
In the embrace, we feel reborn.

Every struggle, a thread so strong,
In this journey, we all belong.
Through the trials, our spirits soar,
Unveiling the bonds forevermore.

Together we rise, no one alone,
In this chorus of hearts, love is known.
Real connections, a beautiful find,
In unveiling the bonds, we intertwine.

Shadows and Light Intertwined

In the dance of dusk and dawn,
Shadows stretch, then softly yawn.
Light embraces, a gentle kiss,
In this union, we find our bliss.

Moments flicker, both dark and bright,
In every heartbeat, a vibrant light.
The night whispers secrets profound,
While the sun's warmth brings laughter around.

In the tapestry of hope and fear,
Both need each other, oh so dear.
From mayhem's depths to calm's delight,
We navigate through shadow and light.

Every storm that stirs the soul,
Is a chance for healing, to become whole.
In every corner, where shadows creep,
The light will cast all darkness deep.

Together they weave a story grand,
In the hug of life, we take our stand.
Shadows and light, forever entwined,
In their embrace, our hearts aligned.

The Pulse of Together

In rhythm we stand, hand in hand,
A heartbeat in sync, a gentle band.
Through stormy nights and bright days,
Together we dance, love's endless ways.

Whispers of dreams shared in the light,
Building our future, a beautiful sight.
Each word a promise, each touch a spark,
In this togetherness, we leave our mark.

Threads of our stories weave and entwine,
Creating a tapestry, you and I combine.
In silent moments, our hearts align,
In this pulse of together, forever we shine.

With laughter and tears, we navigate time,
Every step forward, a rhythm, a rhyme.
Against the world's chaos, we're anchored still,
Our love a fortress, steadfast in will.

From dawn to dusk, our spirits soar,
In the pulse of together, we find our core.
Each heartbeat echoes, a sacred song,
In this harmony, forever we belong.

Hearts Converging

Two souls adrift in the vast sea,
Drawn together by fate's decree.
In the silence, we hear the call,
Hearts converging, breaking the wall.

Like rivers that merge in a graceful flow,
Uncharted paths where we both grow.
In each other's gaze, we find our place,
A gentle embrace, a loving space.

With every whisper, every shared sigh,
Our dreams entwine, reaching the sky.
In laughter's echo, we find our song,
In this dance of love, we both belong.

Through every challenge, side by side,
In this journey together, we take pride.
With hands interlocked, we face the fear,
Hearts converging, forever near.

In the golden dusk of the setting sun,
We feel the warmth; our lives are one.
With every heartbeat, we know it's true,
In this love, forever, me and you.

Whirlwind of Emotions

In the rush of feelings, we often lose track,
A whirlwind of colors, no shades lack.
Joy and sorrow like waves on the shore,
In this great tempest, we keep wanting more.

Fleeting moments, tender and bold,
In this embrace, we both unfold.
Spinning in circles, a dance that we share,
In the whirlwind of emotions, we lay ourselves bare.

The laughter like thunder, the tears like rain,
Together we rise, together the pain.
In the chaos around us, we find our calm,
In this tempestuous journey, love is our balm.

Through every high and the deepening low,
Our hearts are the compass, together we flow.
In the eye of the storm, we find our way,
In this whirlwind of emotions, we choose to stay.

In the quiet aftermath, when silence reigns,
We gather the pieces, release all the chains.
Together we thrive, in this passionate dance,
In a whirlwind of emotions, we seize our chance.

Two Minds, One Thought

In the quiet corners, thoughts intertwine,
Two minds wandering, a path so fine.
With every idea, we effortlessly blend,
In this unity, our spirits transcend.

Conversations woven with threads of gold,
In shared reflections, a story unfolds.
Like stars in the night, our visions align,
Two minds, one thought, our destinies shine.

Through laughter and silence, we spark and ignite,
In this realm of dreams, everything feels right.
With a gentle nudge, we explore what's sought,
In the dance of ideas, wisdom is caught.

In the challenge of choices, we trust and conjoin,
With hope as our guide, we lovingly join.
In a world that is loud, we find solace sought,
In this bond of ours, two minds, one thought.

As seasons shift and the years march by,
Together we grow, reach for the sky.
In the tapestry woven from love's gentle plot,
Forever together, two minds, one thought.

A Journey Beyond Tomorrow

In twilight's glow we set our course,
With dreams that soar, like stars in force.
The dawn awaits with whispers sweet,
A path unknown, where shadows meet.

Through valleys wide, and mountains high,
We chase the clouds that drift and sigh.
Each step reveals a tale untold,
A journey born of courage bold.

The river flows, a silver thread,
With hopes that shine where few have tread.
In every heartbeat, every breath,
We dance with life, defying death.

The compass sways with winds of change,
And yet our hearts will not exchange.
For in this quest, though paths may part,
We carry forth a single heart.

So when the sun dips low and hides,
We'll find our way where love abides.
For every journey leads us home,
Where souls unite, no longer roam.

The Essence of Us

In gentle whispers, love's embrace,
Two hearts entwined, a sacred space.
With every laugh, with every sigh,
We find our truth beneath the sky.

The seasons change, but we remain,
In sunlit joy or softest rain.
Our stories blend, like rivers flow,
In deep communion, we both grow.

Through trials faced, we stand as one,
In darkest nights, we find the sun.
With every touch, a spark ignites,
A flame that warms the coldest nights.

In every glance, a universe,
In every word, a poet's verse.
We paint our world in vibrant hues,
The essence of us, forever true.

As years unfold, like pages turn,
With every lesson, love will learn.
For in the depths, where feelings dwell,
The essence of us is pure and well.

Together in the Whirlwind

Beneath the storm, we find our grace,
In swirling winds, we hold our place.
With laughter bright, we sail the night,
Together strong, we face the fight.

The tempest roars, relentless, wild,
Yet in your eyes, I see the child.
We dance through chaos, hand in hand,
Our spirits rise, like grains of sand.

In fleeting moments, time stands still,
With every heartbeat, stronger will.
We weave a tapestry of dreams,
In vibrant hues, life's joy redeems.

As thunder claps and lightning breaks,
We find the peace that love awakes.
Together, facing what may come,
In every storm, we find our home.

So let the whirlwind swirl around,
In arms of strength, our love is found.
For through the trials, we will soar,
Together, always, forevermore.

Exploring the Heart's Depths

In silent moments, whispers call,
A journey inward, to rise and fall.
With every breath, the soul expands,
In quiet realms, where wisdom stands.

We plunge into the depths of fears,
To face the shadows, shed the tears.
Here, hidden truths begin to gleam,
Awakening from a lost dream.

With eyes wide open, hearts laid bare,
We find the courage to truly care.
The treasures found in darkest night,
Illuminate our way to light.

Each layer peeled reveals the gold,
The stories cherished, gently told.
Through soul's exploration, we embrace,
The beauty found in every space.

For in this journey, love prevails,
As we uncover our true trails.
Exploring deep, we come alive,
In heart's vast depths, together thrive.

Radiance of the Affectionate

In soft light, we find our way,
Hearts entwined, come what may,
Gentle smiles, a warm embrace,
Love's pure glow, in this space.

Through the night, our dreams take flight,
Hand in hand, we chase the light,
With every laugh, with every sigh,
Together, we reach for the sky.

In quiet whispers, our secrets bloom,
Filling each corner, dispelling gloom,
With every moment, our bond does grow,
A radiant warmth, in love's glow.

Past the storms, through the rain,
In the joy, in the pain,
We weave a tapestry, rich and true,
A canvas painted in shades of you.

Time may fade, yet we remain,
In the echoes of love's sweet refrain,
Forever wrapped in affection's light,
Together we'll shine, burn ever bright.

Uncharted Territories of Love

On paths unknown, we set our sails,
Through winding roads and whispered tales,
In every glance, a world we share,
Exploring depths beyond compare.

With open hearts, we brave the night,
Steadfast hope, our guiding light,
Hand in hand, we venture free,
Into the realms of you and me.

In shadows deep, we find our spark,
Creating magic in the dark,
Every heartbeat, a map we trace,
Together forging a sacred space.

Through valleys low and mountains high,
We rise together, you and I,
In every kiss, a treasure unlocked,
An uncharted love, eternally docked.

With every moment, we're writing new,
A story of us, tender and true,
No limits found in love's embrace,
Together, we conquer time and space.

Serendipity Shared

In a glance, our fates aligned,
Moments caught, perfectly timed,
Laughter dances in the air,
Fleeting joy, a love affair.

Like stars that twinkle from afar,
Guiding wishes, our shining star,
In silent echoes, our hearts confide,
The sweet surprise of love's wild ride.

In unexpected gifts, we find delight,
A serendipity that feels just right,
Each turn of fate, a vibrant thread,
Weaving dreams where angels tread.

Through stolen glances, sparks ignite,
In crowded rooms, you're my light,
Every heartbeat writes a story,
Together, we bask in shared glory.

Each day unfolds a new surprise,
A playful twist beneath the skies,
In love's embrace, we'll always stand,
Serendipity, hand in hand.

Whispers of Togetherness

In the hush of night, our voices blend,
Softest secrets, around the bend,
Every whisper, a gentle song,
In this space, we both belong.

Through quiet moments, our hearts converse,
Unraveling the universe,
In every sigh, in every beat,
The pulse of love, endlessly sweet.

With tender touches, we find our way,
Guided by love, come what may,
In every laugh, in every tear,
Together, we conquer doubt and fear.

The world outside may roar and rage,
Yet in our arms, we turn the page,
In silent strength, we stand as one,
Two hearts racing, a life begun.

With every dawn, new dreams arise,
Whispers echo beneath the skies,
In this adventure, side by side,
In love's embrace, we forever abide.

Partners in Time

In the dance of fading light,
We find our steps aligned,
Moments stretching into night,
Two hearts, forever intertwined.

Echoes of laughter fill the air,
Memories softly blend,
With every instant that we share,
Together, we'll transcend.

In the photographs of dreams,
Time is a gentle guide,
Through every flow and stream,
With you, I'm fortified.

As seasons turn, and years unfold,
Our journey comes alive,
In every story yet untold,
It's you for whom I strive.

Partners, we embrace the light,
Hand in hand, we'll roam,
In every star that shines so bright,
Together, we are home.

Beneath the Canopy of Us

Beneath the branches intertwined,
Whispers float on gentle breeze,
Secrets held, in leaves confined,
Time slows down; our hearts at ease.

Sunlight dances on your face,
Nature hums a soothing tune,
In this sacred, quiet place,
We become as one with June.

Every rustle sings our song,
The Earth cradles our embrace,
In this moment, we belong,
Lost in nature's warm embrace.

Together, we weave our dreams,
Amidst the swaying trees,
Here, our love forever beams,
Carried by the softest breeze.

Beneath the canopy above,
Time is a fleeting guest,
In this space, we find our love,
Forever, we are blessed.

Harmonies of Two

In the silence, notes arise,
Melodies of hearts as one,
Softly played beneath the skies,
This symphony's just begun.

Each moment, a rhythmic pulse,
Beating in perfect time,
Together, we find the impulse,
In harmony, we climb.

Voices blend, a sweet refrain,
Chords that echo through the night,
With every joy and every pain,
Our song, a guiding light.

As the world fades into sound,
Whispers fill the gentle air,
In this music, we have found,
A love beyond compare.

Harmonies, they weave and sway,
In this dance, we lose control,
Together, we'll forever play,
Two souls, one timeless whole.

Reflections in an Intimate Mirror

In the stillness of the night,
Your eyes spill stories deep,
Mirrored truths, a wondrous sight,
Awakening thoughts we keep.

Glimmers of joy, shadows of fear,
Intertwined in softest grace,
Every glance, a whispered cheer,
In this most sacred space.

Together, we unravel time,
Every moment, raw and real,
In reflections, thoughts do rhyme,
Creating what we both feel.

As we gaze, we find the past,
In each other's tender gaze,
In this bond, we hold steadfast,
Illuminated by love's blaze.

Intimate mirrors, side by side,
Forever we shall explore,
In shared depths, our hearts abide,
Together, we find more.

The Fire Glows Together

In the warmth of a flickering flame,
We gather close, forgetting the name.
Each spark a whisper, stories to unfold,
Together we shine, our hearts brave and bold.

The night dances softly, a beautiful song,
With shadows that stretch, where we all belong.
Fingers entwined, we share our dreams,
Around this fire, nothing's as it seems.

The crackles echo, like laughter in the air,
A bond unbroken, deep love we share.
As embers fly high, like wishes to the sky,
In this glowing moment, together we fly.

The wood whispers secrets, tales of old,
Our hearts are painted in hues of gold.
Each flame a promise, so tender and true,
In the glow of this fire, I find me and you.

Resonance of Heartbeats

In the stillness, we breathe as one,
Heartbeats softly, like a quiet drum.
Every thump echoes, binding us tight,
In this sacred space, all feels just right.

Your laughter dances, a melody sweet,
Through conversations, our souls meet.
Moments shared, like whispers in the dark,
Together we create, igniting a spark.

Time stands still in this gentle embrace,
Every heartbeat a gift, a tender trace.
We weave our stories, rich tapestry spun,
In the resonance of heartbeats, we are one.

Our dreams intertwine, like vines in the night,
With each pulse, shining ever so bright.
In the rhythm of love, we find our way,
In the resonance of heartbeats, forever we stay.

Murmurs of Together

In soft whispers, secrets unfold,
Murmurs of together, heartbeats bold.
Each word a brushstroke, painting our night,
In the quiet embrace, everything feels right.

The moonlight glimmers, a silver soft glow,
In these gentle murmurs, our spirits grow.
Hand in hand, we wander this way,
In the language of love, words gently sway.

Our laughter circles, like leaves in the breeze,
In these tender moments, we find our ease.
Every glance shared, a universe wide,
In these murmurs of together, there's nowhere to hide.

The night wraps around us, a velvety cloak,
Our dreams take flight, like the last whispered joke.
In this cherished space, we learn to be free,
Murmurs of together, just you and me.

Shared Glances and Smiles

In a crowded room, our eyes first meet,
A silent promise, so pure and sweet.
In shared glances, our worlds collide,
With every smile, deeper bonds abide.

The laughter lingers, like a familiar tune,
In this dance of joy, beneath the moon.
Each moment cherished, a spell unspun,
In shared glances and smiles, we've just begun.

The warmth of friendship, wrapped tight around,
In our silent conversations, love knows no bounds.
Every shared laugh, a memory we weave,
In this playful journey, we learn to believe.

As the night takes flight, like stars on display,
In each shared glance, we find our way.
In smiles exchanged, a bond so divine,
Together forever, your heart next to mine.

A Dance of Souls

In the moon's soft glow, we sway,
A rhythm of whispers, night and day.
Two hearts entwined in a gentle embrace,
Lost in the magic of this sacred space.

With each step taken, the world fades away,
A symphony of breath, we dance and play.
Echoes of laughter, pure as the sky,
In this twilight moment, we learn to fly.

The stars rain down like dreams untold,
A shimmering ballet, both daring and bold.
Hand in hand, through shadows we twirl,
In the dance of souls, our love unfurls.

As night deepens, the music still sings,
In every heartbeat, eternity clings.
Together we forge a path of light,
A dance of souls on this enchanted night.

In silence we know, without any sound,
The beauty of love in each twirl found.
Lost in the rhythm, forever we'll soar,
In the dance of souls, we're always more.

Conversations in Starlight

Beneath the canvas of the night sky,
In whispers of starlight, we dare to fly.
Each twinkle a thought, a secret shared,
A dialogue of dreams, perfectly paired.

The moon smiles gently, a watcher above,
Listening in silence to stories of love.
With every flicker, our souls intertwine,
Conversations in starlight, pure and divine.

We wander through galaxies, thoughts intertwine,
Lost in the glow of a love that's benign.
In the hush of the evening, our voices unite,
Creating a melody that dances in light.

Time pauses gently, as moments unfold,
In conversations so deep, we find hearts of gold.
Every star sparkles with laughter and grace,
In this cosmic dialogue, we find our place.

As dawn approaches, the night softly sighs,
The whispers of starlight fade with the ties.
Yet, in every sunrise, the echoes remain,
Conversations in starlight, a love without chain.

The Gathering of Hearts

In a circle of friends, our laughter rings,
A chorus of joy, in the love that it brings.
The gathering of hearts, a timeless embrace,
Each moment, a treasure, a beautiful trace.

With stories exchanged and spirits set free,
We share bits of life, like leaves on a tree.
In the glow of camaraderie, warmth we find,
A tapestry woven, souls intertwined.

Beneath the vast sky, as daylight gives way,
We dance in the twilight, where shadows play.
In the gathering of hearts, spirits ignite,
A bond that grows stronger, like stars in the night.

Through laughter and tears, we weather the storms,
In each other's presence, our true selves transforms.
The comfort of friendship, a gift that we share,
In the gathering of hearts, love's always there.

As the night deepens, we hold hands so tight,
Grateful for moments that shine ever bright.
In the gathering of hearts, forever we'll stand,
Together as one, in this beautiful land.

Embraced in Silence

In the quiet of night, we find our peace,
Whispers of love, the heart's gentle lease.
Embraced in silence, no words need to flow,
In your arms, I've found a place to know.

Moments like these, soft and profound,
Where time seems to pause, and dreams are unbound.
With a gaze that lingers, we share a calm,
In the stillness of night, love's gentle balm.

Every heartbeat echoes, a silent refrain,
In the embrace of silence, there's no room for pain.
With every breath taken, we create a song,
In a world so loud, our hearts belong.

Underneath the stars, we let our souls blend,
A quiet connection, where love will transcend.
In this serene space, I feel you near,
Embraced in silence, there's nothing to fear.

As dawn's light approaches, I hold you tight,
In the warmth of our bond, everything feels right.
Embraced in silence, forever we'll find,
That love speaks the loudest, in moments confined.

Hearts Aligned

Two souls dance under the moonlight's gleam,
They find a rhythm beyond what we dream.
With every heartbeat a song is played,
In this perfect union, never to fade.

Each glance shared ignites a spark,
In shadows cast, there is no dark.
Hands intertwined, they walk this line,
In gentle whispers, their hearts align.

Through storms that rage and tides that pull,
Together they stand, both brave and full.
With faith as their anchor, love as their guide,
In the symphony of life, they glide side by side.

In laughter and tears, their story unfolds,
A tapestry woven with threads of gold.
They write their chapters in skies above,
Each moment cherished, a testament of love.

As stars bear witness to the vows they've made,
In every heartbeat, their dreams won't fade.
Together they'll face what lies ahead,
With hearts aligned, they forge the thread.

In the Garden of Us

Among blooms bright, our secrets lay,
In whispers soft, we find our way.
Each petal's touch, a promise made,
In the garden of us, love won't degrade.

Sunlight filters through leaves above,
As we nurture the roots of love.
In this sanctuary, time stands still,
Hearts entwined, we cultivate will.

With every season, our bond will grow,
Through winter's frost and summer's glow.
From tender shoots to branches wide,
In the garden of us, we shall abide.

Moments like raindrops, fresh on the ground,
In laughter and joy, harmony found.
As petals fall, new blooms arise,
In this haven, our spirits rise.

Together we tend to dreams that sprout,
In the garden of life, we dance about.
With love as our guide, we'll flourish and thrive,
In the garden of us, forever alive.

Voices in the Silence

In the stillness, whispers rise,
Echoes linger, truth defies.
In quiet moments, we find our song,
Voices in silence, where we belong.

Between the words, our hearts collide,
In unspoken vows, we take our stride.
With gentle sighs, we bridge the space,
In the hush of night, we embrace grace.

Every heartbeat a note of trust,
In the depths of silence, we find what's just.
Beneath the stars, our souls unite,
Voices of love, a guiding light.

In shadows cast, our dreams take flight,
Through veils of quiet, we hold on tight.
In the language of stillness, we seek and find,
Voices in silence, eternally entwined.

With each glance shared, the world recedes,
In the sacred hush, our spirit leads.
Together we journey, hand in hand,
In the whispers of night, we understand.

Merging Destinies

Two paths converge beneath the sky,
With every step, we dare to fly.
In unity's strength, we rise anew,
Merging destinies, just me and you.

In the tapestry of time, we weave,
Every moment a chance to believe.
Fate intertwined, there's no retreat,
With love as the road, our hearts will meet.

Through valleys low and mountains tall,
In victory's dance, we'll rise from the fall.
Together we forge, through shadows and light,
Merging destinies, our spirits ignite.

In every heartbeat, a promise found,
In the music of life, a hopeful sound.
With love as our compass, we journey far,
Merging destinies, like a guiding star.

As the sunsets blaze and dawn draws near,
In this union, there's nothing to fear.
Hand in hand, we chart our course,
Merging destinies, united as one force.

9 789916 891902